W9-BWF-407

34880000 823471

BOOK CHARGING CARD

975.2

Accession No. _____ Call No. CRA

Author _Craats, Rennay_

Title _Maryland_

975.2
CRA

Craats, Rennay
Maryland
34880000 823471

MARYLAND

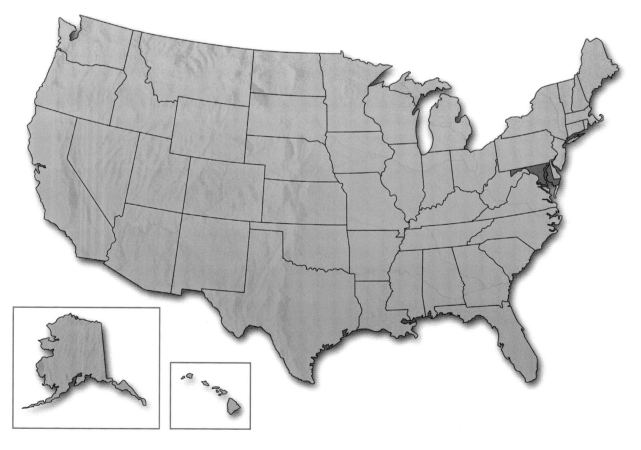

Rennay Craats

Published by Weigl Publishers Inc.
123 South Broad Street, Box 227
Mankato, MN   56002
USA
Web site: http://www.weigl.com

Library of Congress Cataloging-in-Publication Data available upon request from the publisher. Fax: (507) 388-2746 for the attention of the Publishing Records Department.

ISBN 1-59036-000-1

Printed in the United States of America
1 2 3 4 5 6 7 8 9 10   05 04 03 02 01

Editor
Michael Lowry
Designer
Warren Clark
Terry Paulhus
Photo Researcher
Angela Lowen

Photograph Credits
Every reasonable effort has been made to trace ownership and to obtain permission to reprint copyright material. The publishers would be pleased to have any errors or omissions brought to their attention so that they may be corrected in subsequent printings.

Cover: Naval Academy (Middleton Evans), Fishing Nets (Corel Corporation); **Corbis Corporation:** page 29M; **Corel Corporation:** pages 4BL, 10T, 10B, 11T, 11M, 11B, 13B, 14BL, 14BR, 28B; **Middleton Evans:** pages 3T, 3M, 3B, 4T, 4BR, 5T, 6T, 6B, 7T, 7B, 8T, 8B, 9T, 9B, 12T, 12B, 13T, 14T, 15T, 15B, 20T, 21T, 21B, 22T, 22B, 23T, 23B, 24T, 25T, 26T, 26B, 27T, 27B; **Maryland Historical Society:** pages 16T, 16B, 17T, 17B, 18T, 18B, 19T, 19B; **Maryland Tourism/Middleton Evans:** page 20B; **PhotoDisc Corporation:** page 29B; **Photofest:** pages 24B, 25B.

CONTENTS

The United States flag was the inspiration for the national anthem, "The Star-Spangled Banner."

INTRODUCTION

Maryland's mere 12,297 square miles of land features just about all types of natural terrain. Its nickname, "America in Miniature," reflects the wide variety of landscapes that are found in this small state. It also calls attention to Maryland's role in the nation's history. While watching the British attack Baltimore's Fort McHenry, during the War of 1812, Francis Scott Key wrote "The Star-Spangled Banner," making Maryland the birthplace of the National Anthem.

Baltimore, Maryland's largest city, is one of the busiest ports in the country. This leading industrial center is located in Chesapeake Bay, which divides the state into two regions—the Eastern Shore and Western Shore. The warmth and kindness of Marylanders earned Baltimore the nickname "Charm City" and gave the state the reputation as the "Land of Pleasant Living."

QUICK FACTS

Maryland was named after Britain's Queen Henrietta Maria, wife of King Charles I.

"The Star-Spangled Banner" became the official national anthem in 1931. It was written in 1814.

The flag of Maryland honors two important state families—the Calverts and the Crosslands. The black and gold design on the flag represents the Calvert family crest, and the red and white design represents the Crossland family crest.

The Potomac River runs along Maryland's southwestern border.

Since 1951, the Baltimore-Washington International Airport has served more than 246 million commercial passengers.

Getting There

Located on the Atlantic coast, Maryland is one of the most northern of the southern states. Pennsylvania borders Maryland to the north, while Delaware and the Atlantic Ocean form the state's eastern border. Virginia is found to the south and West Virginia to the west.

Access to Maryland is made easy by the 29,313 miles of highway that cross the state. One of the most important roadways is Route 695, which connects to Washington, D.C., in the south and to Philadelphia in the north. International air traffic lands and takes off from the state's biggest airport, the Baltimore-Washington International Airport. For a scenic voyage to Virginia, travelers can also board White's Ferry. This ferry is the last operating ferry crossing the Potomac River. It connects Montgomery County in Maryland to Loudoun County in Virginia.

QUICK FACTS

Most transportation routes in Maryland run through Baltimore.

Maryland is also serviced by two airports in northern Virginia. Both the Dulles International and Washington National airports provide passenger and freight access to the state.

The Chesapeake Bay Bridge first opened in 1952. The bridge links Maryland's Eastern and Western Shores, easing transportation between the two sides of the state.

The state established the first national highway in 1818 and created canals to link waterways in an attempt to improve transportation and shipping. One of America's first railroads was also built in Maryland.

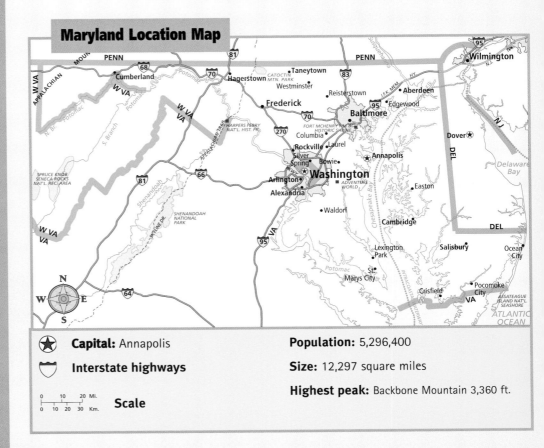

Maryland Location Map

Capital: Annapolis

Interstate highways

Scale

Population: 5,296,400

Size: 12,297 square miles

Highest peak: Backbone Mountain 3,360 ft.

Harborplace is Baltimore's number one tourist destination. The area is home to more than 200 shops and restaurants.

QUICK FACTS

Maryland is the eighth smallest state in the country. It covers 12,297 square miles of land.

At its narrowest point, Maryland is only 1.5 miles wide. A person could walk across the state at this point in less than half an hour.

On April 28, 1788, Maryland became the seventh state to join the Union.

Parts of Washington, D.C., once belonged to Maryland. The District of Columbia was created out of land ceded by Virginia and Maryland.

St. Mary's City was the first capital of Maryland. It was located at the southern tip of the Chesapeake Bay's western shore. In 1694, the capital was moved to Annapolis.

Maryland played an important role in many of the early wars that helped define the United States. During the American Revolution, 400 of the state's soldiers fought off 10,000 British soldiers, helping George Washington's army to escape. This event earned Maryland the nickname "The Old Line State."

Marylanders fought hard to achieve independence for themselves, and for the United States. In 1788, Maryland finally became a state. Its citizens welcomed this new freedom and the new government. Later that year, state leaders established the new American capital near the Potomac River. This area became the District of Columbia in 1791. Since Maryland was largely divided during the American Civil War, and Virginia had joined the Confederacy, the fate of the nation depended on Maryland's wartime decisions. Maryland's Union loyalties ultimately saved Washington, D.C., from being surrendered to the Confederacy.

In 1919, Maryland earned the nickname "The Free State," when Marylanders opposed a law that Congress had passed forbidding the sale and use of alcohol. The belief in state rights and the long tradition of political freedom and religious tolerance makes Maryland truly "The Free State."

St. Mary's City was the fourth permanent British settlement in North America.

In 1884, oyster fishers set a record for the amount of oysters caught in one year—15 million bushels.

While industry boomed in the 1800s, so did the fisheries. The Chesapeake Bay was filled with fish, clams, crabs, and oysters. Oysters by the millions were harvested each year. Fishers commonly brought in 10 million bushels of oysters in a year. Crisfield was the oyster center of the state, and women were important players in this industry. They removed the oysters from the shells, or **shucked** them. The oyster business became very competitive in the region, and oyster wars raged between Maryland and Virginia fishers. It became so serious that fishers began to raid each others oyster beds. Some of these disputes escalated into violent gun fights. Today, oysters are still key elements in the state's economy. Maryland remains one of the top oyster-producing states in the country.

In the twentieth century, Maryland's population soared, and high-technology industries helped the economy to boom. Computers, scientific research, and aerospace became important sectors of the state's economy. By the twenty-first century, Maryland had become one of the wealthiest states in the country.

The blue crab is Maryland's official state crustacean. It was adopted in 1989.

The Piedmont Plateau is covered with low hills and valleys.

LAND AND CLIMATE

Maryland is made up of three main land regions—the Appalachian Mountains, the Piedmont Plateau, and the Atlantic Coastal Plain. The Appalachian Mountains spread across Maryland's western corner. The Piedmont Plateau is a transitional zone that separates the Appalachians from the eastern coast. The state's largest region—the Atlantic Coastal Plain—is flat land ideal for farming.

Maryland's climate is hot and humid in the summer, with an average July temperature of 75° Fahrenheit. Winters in Maryland are mild, with an average temperature in January of 33°F. The western region experiences cooler temperatures than the east. In the west, approximately 46 inches of precipitation falls each year compared to about 38 inches in the east. The majority of the precipitation is rain, but snow is common in winter.

There are more than 600,000 acres of wetlands in Maryland.

NATURAL RESOURCES

One fifth of the total value of all mineral production in Maryland comes from coal.

Important reserves of coal are found in Maryland's Appalachian Mountains. Coal is dug out of large pits called strip mines. Maryland produces about 3.7 million tons of coal each year. Elsewhere in the state, limestone, sandstone, marble, granite, and gravel are mined. These resources are used as building stone and to make roads.

Water is another important natural resource. In Maryland, the boundary between the upland plateau and the coastal plain is called the fall line. Where rivers cross the fall line, waterfalls occur. The power of the falling water is harnessed to produce **hydroelectric** power. The Conowingo Dam on the Susquehanna River is one of the nation's largest hydroelectric plants.

QUICK FACTS

The Chesapeake Bay is the largest **estuary** in North America.

Most of Maryland's electricity comes from thermal plants fueled by coal or oil.

Pennsylvania receives most of the hydroelectric power generated in Maryland.

Maryland's two nuclear plants provide 26 percent of the total electricity output.

The Conowingo Dam is 4,468 feet long and 100 feet high. It was built in 1926.

Maryland has more than 17,000 miles of streams and rivers.

Oak trees can live for more than 200 years.

PLANTS AND ANIMALS

Unlike many other southern states, Maryland's beautiful forests have remained largely intact. Nearly 40 percent of the state is still covered with forests. More than half of the forested area is home to hardwood trees such as oaks and hickories. Black locusts, black cherries, and ash trees are also common in the state. The dominant softwood tree is the loblolly pine. Sweet gum and bald cypress trees flourish in the **wetlands** in the south. The wetlands, which cover about 598,422 acres, are home to thousands of other plants and animals. To the west, hemlock and white pine trees grow in the mountains.

Closer to the ground, dogwood, raspberry, sassafras, and spicebush all grow beneath hardwood trees. Holly, azalea, and huckleberry are also common in these areas. Wildflowers sprout up throughout the state. Mayapple, mountain laurels, golden asters, goldenrods, and black-eyed Susans add a splash of color to Maryland's forests.

QUICK FACTS

Maryland has forty-seven state parks.

The state's official flower is the black-eyed Susan. This bright yellow flower blooms from May until August.

The white oak is the state tree. The largest white oak tree in the country is located in Wye Mills. It stands taller than a ten-story building and is 400 years old.

Azaleas grow best in sunny conditions.

The Delmarva fox squirrel is named after the Delmarva Peninsula where it is found.

The peregrine falcon can be found in the skies near cliffs and bluffs along Maryland's coast. These master hunters can reach speeds of 200 miles per hour as they dive for food.

Bald eagles, robins, blue jays, cardinals, wrens, and mockingbirds all fly Maryland's skies.

House Wren

Ducks, geese, herons, and osprey all spend time in the Chesapeake Bay. Under the water's surface, many freshwater fish, such as trout and catfish, can be found.

Maryland's forests are home to a variety of wildlife, including white-tailed deer, raccoons, foxes, rabbits, skunks, and woodchucks. The Delmarva fox squirrel, an **endangered** species, lives near the Chesapeake Bay. Over-development and competition for food have caused a decline in the number of these animals. They are found in wooded parts of Virginia and Maryland.

The Baltimore oriole, the official state bird, makes its home in Maryland's forests. The orange and black of the male's feathers are similar to the colors on the Calvert shield, so the bird was named after Calvert, or Lord Baltimore.

Hikers need to keep their eyes to the ground, as the state is home to many snakes. The non-venomous green, corn, yellow rat, milk, king, and garter snakes may not cause alarm. However, the venom of copperhead, cotton-mouthed moccasin, and timber rattlesnakes can be dangerous.

Conservationists are trying to reintroduce the peregrine falcon to nesting grounds in Maryland.

Red foxes live throughout the state of Maryland. They eat insects, birds, mice, snakes, nuts, and fruits.

The Maryland Renaissance Festival has been celebrated for more than 25 years.

QUICK FACTS

Crownsville hosts the Maryland Renaissance Festival every year from August to October.

Tourists spend more than $7.5 billion in Maryland every year.

More American soldiers were killed and wounded at the Battle of Antietam than in the American Revolution, War of 1812, Mexican War, and Spanish-American War combined.

Historic Street in St. Mary's City is home to an 800-acre living history museum. The museum contains re-creations of a tobacco plantation, an inn, and one of the first ships that brought settlers to the state.

TOURISM

More than 17 million visitors come to Maryland every year. Many tourists stop off at Ocean City—the state's main seaside resort. Nicknamed "The East Coast's Number One Family Resort," visitors come to relax along its 10 miles of white sandy beaches and to experience the thrill of deep-water sport fishing. In fact, Ocean City is also known as "The White Marlin Capital of the World."

South of Ocean City in the Atlantic Ocean lies the Assateague Island National Seashore. This 37-mile long island is home to herds of wild ponies. Their origin is a mystery. One legend claims that the ponies swam to the island from a shipwrecked Spanish **galleon** in the sixteenth century. Visitors can see the ponies from the island's many trails and beaches.

The Antietam National Battlefield in Sharpsburg stands as a reminder of the bloodiest single battle day in the history of the United States. The Battle of Antietam was one of the most important battles of the Civil War, as Union forces successfully repelled the Confederate invasion of the North. Visitors to the site will learn of the terrible battle of 1862, when 23,000 men were killed or wounded.

About 12,000 people took part in the 1997 re-creation of the Battle of Antietam, and more than 50,000 spectators attended the event.

Shipbuilding is a major industry in Maryland.

INDUSTRY

In the twentieth century, manufacturing has grown to become one of the leading industries in Maryland. In recent years, the state's manufacturing companies have produced more than $36 billion worth of products yearly. Manufactured products in Maryland include food, chemicals, and computer and electronic components. The manufacturing of transportation equipment is also important to the state's economy. One of the main shipbuilding and ship repair yards in the United States is located at Sparrows Point.

One of Maryland's leading manufacturing companies is Black and Decker, based in Towson. Black and Decker is a worldwide manufacturer of power tools, hardware, and other home improvement products. The company operates in 100 countries and has offices established in 14 of them. Black and Decker is well known for its high-quality, innovative products.

QUICK FACTS

The majority of Maryland's manufacturing activity occurs within Baltimore and the surrounding areas.

The Baltimore and Ohio Railroad was founded in Maryland. This company built the first passenger train in the country.

Black and Decker built the drill that NASA astronauts used to remove core samples from the moon.

Baltimore is an important area for the production of metals, such as steel, tin plate, and aluminum.

About 175,000 people are employed in Maryland's manufacturing industry.

In response to customer demands, Black and Decker has created hundreds of different types of drills.

About 162,000 bushels of oysters are harvested from Maryland's waters each year.

GOODS AND SERVICES

Maryland's coastal location makes it a prime center for seafood. Crisfield, on the tip of the eastern shore, is nicknamed the "Seafood Capital of the World" for its abundance of soft- and hard-shelled blue crabs and delicious oysters. Maryland's fishers pull more oysters from their waters than any other state in the country. The state boasts about $63 million each year in seafood **revenues**.

On land, about 2.1 million acres are set aside for farming. Corn, **nursery products**, soybeans, and tobacco are the most valuable agricultural products in Maryland. On the Eastern Shore, vegetable crops are grown and processed. Other valuable crops in the state include barley, oats, wheat, and hay.

Livestock and livestock products account for about 60 percent of Maryland's farm income. Maryland is an important producer of broiler chickens, which account for more than half of the income from livestock. Maryland farmers also raise cows, hogs, and turkeys.

There are about 12,000 farms in Maryland.

QUICK FACTS

While only about 1 percent of Marylanders work in the Chesapeake Bay, its oysters, crabs, fishing, and sailboats have come to identify the state.

About one-quarter of Maryland's farmland is devoted to growing corn.

The state's cows produce about 1.3 billion pounds of milk per year.

Maryland farmers produce more than 290 million broiler chickens per year.

Maryland farmers grow apples, peaches, strawberries, watermelons, and cantaloupes.

The United States Naval Academy was founded on October 10, 1845.

The service industry employs more than half of the state's workers. Many of Maryland's service employees work in Washington, D.C. These employees include federal government employees and military personnel. Some of the major institutions include the National Institutes of Health, the Census Bureau, and the Goddard Space Flight Center. Scientists and engineers at the flight center are devoted to the study of Earth from space. It is the largest research team of its kind in the world.

Maryland has the best educated work force in the country. One third of the population over the age of 25 has a bachelor degree or higher. The Johns Hopkins University, in Baltimore, has one of the best medical schools and is one of the most **prestigious** research facilities in the country. The state is also home to the United States Naval Academy. Located in Annapolis, the academy is responsible for training students to be officers in the United States Navy and the United States Marine Corps.

Founded in 1876, the Johns Hopkins University was the first research university in the United States.

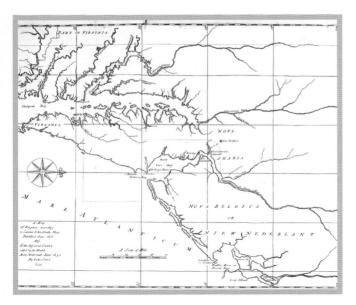

Early European explorers used Native-American words to name rivers and towns in the Maryland area.

FIRST NATIONS

By the early seventeenth century, many Native-American groups could be found living around the Chesapeake Bay. The majority of the groups belonged to the Algonquian family—this included the Conoy and Patuxent in the west and the Choptank, Nanticoke, Assateague, and Pocomoke in the east. An Iroquois group, the Susquehannock, settled along the Susquehanna River.

The Native Peoples in Maryland traveled the region in search of food and did not establish permanent villages. They hunted deer and other animals and fished the waterways. They also traded blankets and food with other Native-American groups. As Europeans began to settle in the region, most of the Native Peoples moved away. Those who stayed often fought with the settlers over land. They also battled against the new diseases brought by Europeans.

The name *Susquehannock* means "people of the muddy river." The Susquehannock were farmers, fishers, and hunters.

King Charles I of England granted the charter for the colony of Maryland to Lord Baltimore in 1632.

QUICK FACTS

Originally, the area was called "Mariland." The spelling was later changed to "Maryland."

Cecilius Calvert inherited his father's desire to settle North America, as well as the title of Lord Baltimore.

Leonard Calvert and the settlers arrived in Maryland aboard two ships—the *Ark* and the *Dove*.

EXPLORERS AND MISSIONARIES

The first Europeans in Maryland were Italian. Giovanni da Verrazano sailed through the Chesapeake Bay in 1524. However, he did not land in the area. In 1608, John Smith, the founder of a colony in Virginia, became the first European to map the bay. At this time, explorers from England were reaching North America and claiming the shores for their king. Much of Maryland's coast, including the Chesapeake Bay, was claimed by the English. In 1632, Britain's King Charles I gave part of the Chesapeake Bay area to George Calvert, also known as Lord Baltimore, and named the area Maryland in honor of the queen.

Lord Baltimore wanted to establish a colony where Catholics could worship without the **persecution** they faced in England. He died before the deal was completed, and his son Cecilius took over the effort. Cecilius sent his brother Leonard to North America with about 200 settlers.

Baltimore was founded as a trading center. It was named in honor of Lord Baltimore.

EARLY SETTLERS

Cecilius, now known as Lord Baltimore, and his brother Leonard Calvert claimed the south bank of the Potomac River up to the fortieth parallel, as well as most of the Delmarva Peninsula. Leonard and the settlers arrived in Maryland in 1634 at Saint Clements Island. They founded St. Mary's City in an old Native-American village. The settlers built houses, a fort, and a church. They farmed the land that the Native Peoples had cleared.

At first, the settlers enjoyed good harvests and established strong relations with the Native Peoples in the area. The Native Peoples traded furs and food for **textiles** and tools. They also helped the settlers grow corn. This knowledge prevented the European newcomers from starving. The settlers also grew tobacco, which they sold to England. Using the money they made selling tobacco, the settlers established **plantations** to grow even more of the crop.

Cecilius Calvert, the second Lord Baltimore, never visited Maryland.

Early tobacco plantations in Maryland were very profitable, and many citizens became wealthy from the sale of tobacco.

As tobacco plantations spread across the Maryland region, the Native-American groups in the area were forced to relocate. More and more settlers arrived. The British settlers were joined by French colonists. In the mid-1700s, the two countries went to war for control of the region. To pay for the war, Britain taxed settlers heavily on goods imported from Europe, including sugar, tea, and newspapers. This angered the settlers, and they stopped buying whatever they could from Britain.

The high taxes also pushed the settlers to fight for independence from Britain. The settlers wanted to have total control over their affairs. By 1776, the American Revolution had swept across the country. While Maryland did not see much fighting, a group of soldiers called the Maryland Line represented the region by joining the Continental Army. In 1776, Marylanders announced their independence, and four representatives from the area signed the Declaration of Independence.

General McClellan led Union troops against a Confederate invasion of Maryland during the American Civil War.

General Ross was killed by the 3rd Brigade of Maryland Militia, when the British marched on Baltimore during the Battle of North Point in the War of 1812.

More than 90 percent of Maryland's population lives in the state's five metropolitan areas.

POPULATION

For such a small state, Maryland has a large population. The state's population is about 5.3 million people, making it the nineteenth most-populated state in the country. There are an average of 542 people for every square mile of land in the state. This is one of the highest population densities in the country. In comparison, California, which boasts the highest population in the country, has a population density of only 72 people per square mile. About 80 percent of Maryland's population lives along a strip of land that runs between Baltimore and Washington, D.C.

Maryland also maintains a strong rural tradition, especially in the southern and western parts of the state. The smaller cities and towns in these areas enjoy many of the conveniences of larger cities while maintaining the easy pace of rural communities.

Baltimore is one of the major port cities in the United States. It has a population of about 650,000 people.

QUICK FACTS

The five most populated cities in Maryland are Baltimore, Dundalk, Rockville, Frederick, and Hagerstown.

Some Maryland communities are made up of only a small number of families.

Construction of Maryland's State House, in Annapolis, was begun in 1722 and completed in 1779.

POLITICS AND GOVERNMENT

Maryland's State House is the oldest State Capitol still in use. For 200 years, the state's government representatives have made important decisions in this historic building.

Today's government is made up of three branches. The legislative branch creates the laws for the state. The 47 members of the Senate and the 141 members of the House of Delegates make up this branch. The executive branch ensures that the laws are followed. The governor heads the executive branch and works alongside the lieutenant governor, the secretary of state, and the attorney general. The judicial branch interprets the laws through the courts. There are twelve district courts and eight circuit courts. The state's highest court is the Court of Appeals.

QUICK FACTS

Maryland has forty-seven legislative districts. Voters in each of these districts elect one senator and three delegates during elections.

There are twenty-three counties in Maryland. Most counties are governed by a commissioner or council. Baltimore is considered an independent city and is not part of a county. Maryland is one of only two states in the country with an independent city.

Lawyer Thurgood Marshall was born in Baltimore. He fought for African-American rights and became the first African-American judge on the United States Supreme Court in 1967.

Government House, in Annapolis, has been the home of Maryland's governors since 1870.

CULTURAL GROUPS

While many Marylanders are of English and French **ancestry**, settlers from other countries began coming to the region in the 1700s. Germans settled near Frederick and then Baltimore in 1734. They established a Lutheran church and the communities worked to protect the German culture. Marylanders still celebrate traditional German customs and festivals.

Baltimore is a very **diverse** city. It is made up of people from Italy, Ireland, Poland, and Russia. Czechs, Greeks, and Jews also call Baltimore home. Ethnic neighborhoods throughout the city preserve their culture's heritage and identity. The residents of these neighborhoods invite others to experience their cultures through shops, museums, theaters, and restaurants.

There are about 188,000 Asian-Americans living in Maryland.

QUICK FACTS

Descendants of some of Maryland's earliest settlers still live on Smith Island.

Maryland was known as an area of religious freedom. Many different religious groups, such as Quakers, Methodists, and Presbyterians, settled in the area so they could worship freely.

Creole and Cajun culture is celebrated every year with the Gumbo Jam. This New Orleans-style festival presents tasty authentic cuisine, as well as Cajun and **Zydeco** music.

Other festivals in Maryland include the Greek Festival, the Baltimore Irish Festival, the Hispanic Festival, and the Reggae Wine Festival.

Greek people in Maryland celebrate their culture with traditional costumes and dance.

There are approximately 20,000 Native Americans living in Maryland today.

The arrival of immigrants to the state has offset the departure of Marylanders to other areas in the United States. Many of these newcomers have arrived from Asian and Latin-American countries, adding richness to the cultural mosaic of the state.

The African-American community is strong in Maryland. More than half of Baltimore's population and about 28 percent of the state's total population is African American. The Kunta Kinte Heritage Festival in Annapolis is a celebration of African-American culture. Africans, African Americans, and African Caribbeans join together to highlight their fascinating history, culture, and heritage. Visitors can take part in a wide variety of activities, such as storytelling, dancing, singing, and mask-making.

Maryland hosts the American Indian Inter-Tribal Cultural Powwow each summer. This event celebrates traditional dancing, singing, crafts, and food. The Howard County Powwow and the American Indian Festival are other summer festivals that present Native-American arts and entertainment.

Since the Kunta Kinte Heritage Festival began in 1989, more than 125,000 people have visited Annapolis to learn about African traditions.

QUICK FACTS

Eastern Shore residents have many phrases that can confuse visitors. A "blue hen's chicken" is not a chicken at all but a wild young person. "Little nicks" are small clams, and "taut as a tick" is what Eastern Shore residents say after they eat a large meal.

The Kunta Kinte Heritage Festival was named after a character in Alex Haley's novel *Roots*. The book follows the story of an African man who was sold into slavery.

ARTS AND ENTERTAINMENT

The Walters Art Museum, in Baltimore, is named after its founders Henry and William Walters.

Maryland has produced many brilliant authors. Born in Baltimore in 1947, Tom Clancy published his first novel, *The Hunt for Red October*, in 1984. The books that followed were suspenseful thrillers that combined modern technology and the world of politics. In 1997, he became the highest-paid author in the United States by signing a $100-million contract.

Dashiell Hammett is another well-known novelist. His detective stories, such as *The Maltese Falcon* and The Thin Man series, thrilled and captivated readers. His main character, Sam Spade, became a national hero and appeared in many popular films. Hammett was born in St. Mary's County in 1894.

Marylanders interested in art can visit the Baltimore Museum of Art, which is one of the largest museums in the country. It has on display more than 85,000 objects from around the world and boasts 50,000 books and magazines in its library.

QUICK FACTS

The Walter Arts Museum art collection contains pieces from ancient Egypt through to modern Europe.

The Havre de Grace Decoy Museum displays wooden hunting decoys. Decoys help hunters attract waterfowl. Making decoys has become an art form.

Baltimore author Upton Sinclair wrote more than ninety books, several plays, and countless articles. He drew attention to important social issues.

Anne Tyler set many of her novels in Baltimore. In 1989, she won the Pulitzer Prize for *Breathing Lessons*.

Tom Clancy's novels have inspired several movies and video games.

The Baltimore Symphony Orchestra was founded in 1916.

Classical music lovers in Maryland flock to the Meyerhoff Symphony Hall, in Baltimore, to listen to the Baltimore Symphony Orchestra and Chorus or to the Lyric Opera House to catch current presentations. The Maryland Hall for the Creative Arts, in Annapolis, showcases a variety of performing arts including classical music, opera, and ballet.

Many non-classical musicians have also called Maryland home. Early in the twentieth century, Baltimore's Eubie Blake made important contributions to music. He was one of the first musicians to develop and popularize a music style called "ragtime." This style, created mostly for piano, accented or stressed unusual beats in songs. This introduced a completely different sound to the nation's music lovers. Blake wrote many ragtime hit songs, including "I'm Just Wild About Harry" and "Memories of You."

Billie Holiday is considered a jazz icon and one of the most popular jazz musicians of all time. While she made her mark in New York City in the late 1920s, she never forgot her Baltimore home. Holiday's music influenced musicians for decades to come, and her beautiful singing style was often imitated but rarely matched.

Billie Holiday's real name is Eleanora Fagan Gough.

SPORTS

For sports-minded Marylanders, there is always something to do in the state. Jousting is an unusual sport that is popular with Marylanders. It dates back hundreds of years and is Maryland's official state sport. In modern jousting contests, competitors race their horses down a 100-yard track and capture three rings with their lances.

Horses play an important role in another Maryland pastime—horse racing. The Preakness, held in Baltimore, is one of the greatest racing events in the country. It is one of the three horse races in the country that make up the prestigious **Triple Crown**.

For a fast-paced, exciting sport, many Marylanders turn to lacrosse. Lacrosse players use a stick with a netted basket at the end and try to shoot a rubber ball past a goalie into a net. College lacrosse teams battle for the championship each year. The lacrosse teams from Johns Hopkins University and the University of Maryland are some of the best in the country.

There are about fifty jousting competitions, or "ring tournaments," in Maryland each year.

QUICK FACTS

In 1962, Maryland became the first state in the country to adopt a state sport—jousting.

The first successful hot-air balloon flight in the United States took off from Maryland in 1784. The basket carried a 13-year-old boy from Baltimore.

The Lacrosse Hall of Fame is located at Johns Hopkins University in Baltimore.

Many former University of Maryland lacrosse players have gone on to professional lacrosse careers.

In 2000, Cal Ripken, Jr. swatted his 3,000th hit and 400th home run.

QUICK FACTS

Great Maryland baseball players include Babe Ruth, Lefty Grove, Frank Baker, and Jimmie Foxx.

Other popular sports teams from Maryland include the Baltimore Blast soccer team, the Baltimore Bayhawks lacrosse team, and the Baltimore Burn women's football team.

Johnny Unitas was the star quarterback for the Baltimore Colts for sixteen years. During that time, he brought three Super Bowl titles home to Maryland. He was inducted into the Pro Football Hall of Fame in 1979.

Oriole Park has open stands and real grass, just like old-fashioned baseball stadiums.

Cal Ripken, Jr. was the league's Most Valuable Player (MVP), the All-Star MVP, and Player of the Year in 1991.

There are several professional sports teams that keep Marylanders cheering, but the Baltimore Orioles are the state's sweethearts. The team has been a part of Major League Baseball since 1954. Top players, including Delino DeShields, Brady Anderson, and Mike Bordick, keep the Orioles in the pennant race. Cal Ripken, Jr. captured the sporting world's attention with both his incredible talent and his loyalty. From 1982 until 1998, he did not miss a game, setting a record of 2,632 consecutive games. Ripken continued to wow fans with his home runs and amazing fielding until his retirement after the 2001 season.

In 1984, the Baltimore Colts professional football team left Maryland for Indianapolis. Fans were crushed. The team had won the Super Bowl in 1971. But football could not stay away from Maryland. In 1996, professional football returned with the Baltimore Ravens. To celebrate the return of professional football, the city opened a new stadium in 1998 beside Oriole Park at Camden Yards. In 2001, the Ravens won the Super Bowl by triumphing over the New York Giants by a score of 34 to 7.

The PSINet Stadium, in Baltimore, is the home of the Baltimore Ravens. The stadium can seat more than 69,000 fans.

Brain Teasers

1

Why is Oriole Park different from most baseball parks?

Answer: Unlike most modern stadiums, Oriole Park was built exclusively to host baseball games. Most arenas are built to accommodate other sports teams, concerts, or special events as well.

2

Which well-known Marylander was nicknamed "The Sultan of Swat"?

Answer: George Herman "Babe" Ruth, Jr. Babe Ruth was born in Baltimore and went on to become one of the greatest home-run hitters in baseball history.

3

What happened to the ship *Peggy Stewart*?

Answer: Marylanders were angry about the high taxes placed on British goods. *Peggy Stewart*, which was carrying 2,000 pounds of British tea, was set on fire in the Annapolis harbor in protest.

4

What was nicknamed the "Iron Horse"?

Answer: The Baltimore and Ohio Railroad steam-powered engine, which was to travel along one of the first railroads in the country, was nicknamed the "Iron Horse." It raced against a real horse to see which was faster. The real horse won the race.

5

Which Maryland event is known as "The 11 Best Days of Summer"?

Answer: The Maryland State Fair. The first state fair was held in 1878. The fair is held at the end of August in Timonium.

6

Whose consecutive game record did Cal Ripken, Jr. beat?

Answer: In 1995, Ripken played in his 2,131st game. This beat Lou Gehrig's 2,130-game record.

7

Where can you go to view George Washington's teeth?

Answer: The Dr. Samuel D. Harris National Museum of Dentistry in Baltimore has on display a pair of George Washington's dentures. Maryland is also home to the first dental school in the United States. The school was founded in 1840 at the University of Maryland.

8

Which Baltimore building contains more than 1 million gallons of water?

Answer: The National Aquarium in Baltimore. The aquarium is home to more than 10,000 marine and freshwater animals.

FOR MORE INFORMATION

Books

Colbert, Judy. *Maryland and Delaware.* Guilford, CT: Globe Pequot Press, 1999.

Johnson, Joyce. *Hello U.S.A.: Maryland.* Minneapolis: Lerner Publications Company, 1991.

Reger, James P. *The Battle of Antietam.* Battles of the Civil War Series. San Diego: Lucent Books, 1997.

Web Sites

You can also go online and have a look at the following Web sites:

Maryland Tourism
http://www.mdisfun.org

Maryland Information
http://www.portaltomaryland.com

Inner Harbor
http://www.baltimore.to/baltimore.html

Some Web sites stay current longer than others. To find other Maryland Web sites, enter search terms such as "Maryland," "Antietam," "Baltimore," or any other topic you want to research.

GLOSSARY

ancestry: family line; descendants from whom an individual or group is descended

diverse: made up of different kinds

endangered: at risk

estuary: the part of a river where it meets the sea, and fresh and salt water mix

galleon: a large sailing ship used between the fifteenth and seventeenth centuries

hydroelectric: using waterpower to create electricity

nursery products: commercially grown plants

persecution: harsh treatment because of religious or political beliefs

plantations: large estates that grow crops such as cotton, tea, and tobacco

prestigious: something that brings respect, power, success, or a good reputation

revenues: annual incomes

shucked: to have removed the shell of an oyster or clam

textiles: fabrics made by weaving or knitting

Triple Crown: the title held by the horse that wins the three most important horse racing events in the United States—the Kentucky Derby, the Belmont Stakes, and the Preakness Stakes

wetlands: swamps and marshes

Zydeco: a blues-influenced style of dance music

INDEX